Under Fire

by
Mir Tamim Ansary

Staff Credits: Joshua Adams, Melania Benzinger, Karen Blonigen, Laura Chadwick, Andreea Cimoca, Katie Colón, Nancy Condon, Barbara Drewlo, Kerry Dunn, Marti Erding, Sara Freund, Daren Hastings, Ruby Hogen-Chin, Mariann Johanneck, Julie Johnston, Mary Kaye Kuzma, Mary Lukkonen, Carol Nelson, Carrie O'Connor, Marie Schaefle, Julie Theisen, Chris Tures, Mike Vineski, Charmaine Whitman, Sue Will

ISBN-13: 978-0-7854-6689-5

ISBN-10:   0-7854-6689-4

1 2 3 4 5 6 7 8 9 10   12 11 10 09 08

1-800-992-0244
www.pearsonschool.com

Contents

1. Ana

Will pulls up to the building and then just sits for awhile, looking at the front of it. The name of the place is over the door in red letters: Sea House. To eat at this place, you need a lot of money. The Sea House is one of the better restaurants on the north side of town.

Will gets out and opens up the back of his truck. Cool air hits him in the face. The truck was made to hold frozen fish and meat. Only two boxes are left this late in the day. Both go here to the Sea House.

Will works for Mississippi Meat and Fish—MMF for short. He takes fish and meat around to different restaurants. MMF is not a fancy place. The building is little more than a big box down by the water. The outside walls used to be white, but you wouldn't know it anymore. The inside is clean, but again—not fancy. Everyone—even the boss—comes to work in jeans. The boss is a short man called Lou. Will doesn't know his last name—no one seems to. "Lou," he tells everyone. "Just call me Lou." That is his way of showing that he is one of the guys. Lou came up the hard way, and he never lets anyone forget it. But he does have his own room in the corner of the building. It is up some stairs and has big windows. Through the glass, Lou keeps a close eye on his workers.

Will works every day after school. Every day he gets to the MMF building around 3:00 PM. Lou gives him his **card** for the day. The card tells Will where to go that day and how many boxes of meat or fish (or both) to take to each place. Most days Will finds about 12 restaurants on his card.

Will has to get the boxes and put them on the truck. When he gets to each restaurant, he has to take out the right boxes and get them to the kitchen. Some places want him to take the boxes right into a walk-in freezer. This is not really part of his job, but he is happy to do it. Some places tell him to just leave the boxes by the door. This takes up only a small part of Will's time. Most of what he does at work is drive. He has to get from one restaurant to another, and they are all over the north side.

Someday Will would like to get a better job and make more money. This job is OK for now. Will likes driving a truck. He doesn't mind moving big boxes. He thinks of it as working out. Will can start after school and be back home in time for dinner. These are all good things.

The money is not bad for a guy in his last year of high school. Will makes enough to take his girlfriend out. He couldn't take her to a fancy place like the Sea House, but he could take her to the Short Stop where he and his friends like to hang out. After dinner, they could go hear a little music somewhere.

The trouble is Will doesn't have a car. He has to leave the truck at MMF when he gets off work. Without a car, how can he take a girl out? On the bus? People might laugh at him. Or the girl might look down on him. Will just couldn't stand something like that.

That's why Will does his best to save money. Every week he puts away as much as he can. He now has about $400 in the bank. It's not enough, of course—not even close. Even a used car will set him back $1,000 or more. But Will knows he's getting there.

The car, however, is only one problem. When it comes to taking his girlfriend out, Will has another problem, too. He doesn't have a girlfriend. There is a girl he thinks about a lot. Her name is Ana. She works at the Sea House. Sometimes she says "hi" to him as he goes by, and he gets a strong feeling that she likes him. On those days, he goes home feeling like he could walk on air. Other days, she doesn't even look up. If he says "hi," she doesn't answer. He gets the feeling she doesn't even know that he's alive. On those days, he goes home feeling bad. Will would like to stop and talk to Ana someday, but he doesn't know what he would say. So he just smiles at her and moves on past.

Will knows he will see her today. She is always here at this time. This is why Will always tries to make the Sea House his last stop. He wants to be there at the same time as Ana. He stops to look through the kitchen window. Will can see Ana way in the back washing dishes. That's only one of her jobs. Ana does a lot of things at the Sea House. She gives the cook a hand at times. She even helps Mrs. White count the money at night. Fannie White runs the place for Mr. Henson, the owner.

The head cook is a guy by the name of Matthew. He seems to think of himself as some kind of star. Most people find him good-looking, but not Will. Will doesn't like him at all. He doesn't know why, but there is just something about the man.

Today as he gets the door open, he hears Matthew call out to Ana. "Hey, you! Did you get that fish ready for me yet?"

Ana looks at him. "Yes. But my name is Ana. I don't like to be called **you**."

"Oh. You don't? You're fired!" Then Matthew starts to laugh. He turns to his helper, who is standing next to him. "Get it? She's fired!" He turns back to Ana. "Not really. What's wrong with you? Lose the long face, girl! I want only happy people working around me. That goes for all of you." He turns slowly to look at all the workers. "If you want to work in this kitchen, learn to laugh! Anyone who doesn't crack up when I tell a joke is fired." Matthew laughs. No one else does. "You're all fired," says Matthew. "Just kidding. But Ana, hey, you know I like you. I wouldn't kid you if I didn't. Just to prove it, I'll take you out one of these days. I have a boat. We'll go out on the water and take some food along. I'll let you know when."

Ana doesn't look up. "I am needed at home that day."

"But I didn't say which day—oh, I get it. Big laugh, Ana. What a card. You and me, we make a set," says Matthew. "We'll talk about this later."

Suddenly, Will knows what he doesn't like about Matthew. It's the way he kids people. He finds the one thing someone feels bad about. Then he makes one joke after another about it. Ana doesn't like the kidding. Will can see that. Why can't Matthew?

Will walks into the kitchen. "Hi, Ana."

"Hi, Will." She keeps on working. Well, she knows his name—that's good. But as always, she has no more to say to him. That's how it always goes with Ana. But then, Will thinks, *a girl as pretty as Ana must have a boyfriend. Maybe that's why she keeps to herself so much.*

He takes the box of fish past Ana to the back of the kitchen. The freezer door is shut. "Matthew," he calls out, "you want me to leave the fish here or what?"

"Put it in the freezer, boy. What's wrong with you? Don't you know your own job?"

Matthew is not much older than Will—maybe six years at the most. What gives him the right to call Will **boy**? Will doesn't like it. Anyway, putting the fish into the freezer is not really Will's job. He's done it in the past just to help out. But it's not worth fighting about. Will pulls the freezer door open and goes inside. Just as he puts the box down, the door starts to shut. Will races back to get it. He sure doesn't want to get locked in the freezer. *I should take a close look at that door,* he thinks as he goes for the other box. *I should see where the inside handle is and how it works.*

This time as he walks past Ana, he says, "How are things?"

She says, "All right." She keeps on working. She is trying to get some food off a dish. The food has been cooked on hard, so she has to really work at it. Her arms and face are dirty.

Even now she looks so pretty. *I should ask her out,* Will thinks. *What am I waiting for?* So on his way back from the freezer, he stops next to Ana. He says, "I was thinking—"

"What's that?" She looks up from her work. "Oh, Will. Yes? Did you want something?"

Will says, "You don't really know me, so I was thinking—well, the fact is I don't know you that well either, so—"

"Will, what are you trying to say?"

"Well, I'm trying to ask a question. How can two people ever get to know each other, you know? We say 'hi' to each other all the time. But I guess you hear this kind of thing all the time. If this is out of line, just let me know."

"If **what** is out of line?" Her eyes fix on his.

Will feels lost. She **must** know that he is trying to ask her out. Maybe this is just her way of telling him to get lost. "What I'm trying to say is—"

Just then Ana's boss, Mr. Henson, walks into the kitchen. Mr. Henson, the owner, stops in sometimes to make sure everyone is working hard. "Ana!" he says. "Do I pay you to work or talk to boys?"

"Work, Mr. Henson." Ana gives Will a look.

"We'll talk some other time." Will heads for the back door. He doesn't want to leave yet, but what can he do? Outside the sun has set. The street is getting dark, and the air feels cold. *A storm is coming,* Will thinks, as he looks up at the sky. He feels like a storm is coming inside him, too. He likes that girl. If only she would like him, too!

2. The Sick Dogs

After dinner that night, Will picks up his guitar and heads down the street to see his friend, Robert.

"Hey, Will," says Robert as he opens the door. "What's happening, man?"

"Nothing much. Same old," says Will. "You?"

"Sitting around with Jared and Mark. Come in."

"Oh, are they here, too?" Will follows Robert down the stairs to his room. He waves to the other two. "What's happening, boys?"

"Meeting of the band?" Jared smiles.

The band is a joke with these guys. They all like music, and for years now they have been getting together to play. But they just do it to have a good time. They know they're not really a band. Oh, they play for friends now and again. One time they played at a school social. But they have never played for people they don't know. Sometimes they joke about getting jobs as a band, but they know they are not good enough. Who would pay to hear them? Still the joke keeps coming up. These days, they sometimes forget to laugh.

"Jared is right," says Robert. "We're all here, and Will has his guitar. Why don't we play some music? I was writing a song today. Does anyone want to hear it?"

"You?" laughs Jared.

"Why not me? I didn't say it was a **great song**, just a song."

"Hey, that's cool, Robert," says Will. "Did you write down the words?"

"Sure did. Here. You guys read along as I sing it." Robert runs through his song a few times, and after that his friends join in. The song is about a girl. Will likes the feeling it gives. The words are sad, but in a good way. They make him think of Ana.

"You never see me at all,
Never know I'm there.
I love you more than all the world,
Girl—how come, how come you don't care?"

Yes, thinks Will. *That's just how it is. She doesn't even know I'm there!* Suddenly his hands are on fire. He can turn his feelings right into music. He takes off on a guitar break. The other guys back him up, give him space, and let him burn. Soon Will is flying. At last, something tells him it is time to come back. He drives his guitar back to Earth and lands just where he took off. Robert has a big smile on his face, and his eyes are closed. He starts to sing again. A thought races through Will's mind. *Tonight we **are** a band.*

When the song ends, no one says anything at first. Then Mark laughs. "All right! We were hot!"

"I think we're ready," Robert smiles. "Will, how about you and I go down to the Green Spider and get us a job?"

"No can do," says Will. "Whoever heard of a band with no name?"

"**That** could be our name: **Band With No Name**."

"How about: Band With No Singer," says Mark. He gives Robert a smile. "Don't take this wrong, Robert—great song. But you do sound like a sick dog."

"And so do you," Jared tells Mark.

"And so do I," Will tells them all.

Robert says, "And so do all of us."

"I have an idea for a name," says Jared. "How about **The Sick Dogs**? Every band needs some little thing to set it apart. Our thing could be that we can't sing."

"Oh, that should pull people in," says Robert.

Will sets his guitar down and sits back. "You know that is our big problem. We need a singer. Me—I need a new guitar. This old thing has a crack in it."

"I know where you can pick up a new guitar for next to nothing," says Robert. "A guy tried to sell one to me the other day. I turned him down. This is where you can reach him, if you're interested." Robert hands over a paper on which he has written: 555–7670.

Will takes the paper, then shakes his head. "I'm not buying a stolen guitar."

"How about buying a new one?" asks Robert. "Don't you have a job now?"

"Yes, but I have to save my money. I need a car even more than a new guitar," says Will.

Jared says, "How are we going to play at the Green Spider if you don't get a new guitar?"

All the boys laugh. "I don't know," says Will. "I guess the world isn't going to hear from The Sick Dogs anytime soon."

3. The Cook

Will can hardly wait to see Ana again—but he has to. He can't go back to the Sea House till they put in an order. While he waits, he thinks about how to handle his next meeting with Ana. Just "hi" won't cut it anymore. He has to have a longer talk with her. But when? Mr. Henson will get mad if he tries to talk to her when she's working.

Then he remembers something. Ana takes a break between 6:30 and 7:00. Of course, that **is** a little late. Most days, Will is getting back to MMF around 6:30. Maybe he can push it just one time.

On the last day of that week, the Sea House orders six boxes of frozen meat. Will takes his time that day. So it is just 6:30 when he pulls up to the restaurant. Parked just ahead of him is a fancy red car. *Must be some rich guy inside*, he thinks.

He goes in through the back door. The kitchen feels hot. The orders are coming in fast. Matthew's main helper is working hard over the heat. He keeps passing dish after dish through a window. "Order up!" he cries. "Order up!" Matthew stands by, looking on.

Suddenly Mr. Henson comes along. "What are you doing here?" he cries out.

"I have your boxes of frozen meat."

"Who told you to come now? You should get here before 6:00! People are eating. You can't truck boxes through the restaurant now! Are you out of your mind?"

"I was going to use the back door. I'm sorry. I guess I'm running a little late today." Will leaves the sentence hanging. He has just seen Ana walking toward the back. "It won't happen again," Will says.

"All right," says Mr. Henson. "Do what you have to. Just do it fast."

Will goes out to get the boxes of meat. He has to take them in one by one today. He picks up the first one and starts toward the restaurant. Then he sees two people standing by the back door. One of them is Ana. The other is Matthew, the cook.

They are talking. The sun has set, but the street lights have not come on yet, so the light is poor. Even so, Will can see that something is going on. He stops, not knowing what to do. He would have to walk right between them to get to the restaurant. He doesn't think he should break in on them like that. He even feels it's wrong to watch them, but he can't help himself. He wants to know what is happening. He just stands there with the box of frozen meat against his body. Matthew is doing most of the talking. He seems to be asking for something. Will can't hear the words, but he can see Ana shake her head. Matthew asks again. Again, Ana shakes her head. She starts to go inside. The cook stops her.

"Let go of my arm," says Ana.

Will doesn't like the sound of that. He moves closer.

"Is that any way to talk to a friend?" Matthew laughs, but he doesn't sound friendly.

"I don't want to hurt your feelings," says Ana. "But—"

"You couldn't hurt my feelings. Listen. I'll take you to some really fancy place. Anywhere you like—just name it. I have lots of money. See?"

He pulls some bills out of his pocket to show her. A few of them fall to the ground, and he just leaves them there, as if they mean nothing.

"I have nothing to wear to a fancy place," says Ana.

"Oh, is that the problem? Go buy yourself something pretty. I'll pay for it. Hey, I wouldn't take you out looking like you do right now anyway. If you look bad, I look bad. Know what I mean?"

"No, Matthew. You don't get it. I just don't want to go out with you."

Matthew's face turns hard. "You must be kidding! You think you're the only fish in the sea? A lot of girls would love to be in your place."

"Good. Ask one of them."

Matthew moves closer to Ana. His eyes, in that darkness, look a little red. "You're the one who doesn't get it. I'm a guy with money. I'm a guy with class. Didn't you see my new car out front, the red one? I'm going places. I got written up in the paper again today. The paper said: **Up and Coming Cook Matthew Makes Sea House One of the Best**. Didn't you see it? This town is going to be at my feet. I don't need you—you need me."

Just then the street lights go on. The cook sees him and calls out. "Hey, Will! Get over here. I need you to help me make a point."

"Don't listen to him," says Ana. "You have work to do."

"This won't take long," says Matthew. "I just want Ana to take a good look at you." He turns back to Ana. "See Will here? Turn me down, and you could end up with a guy like him. Some kid who trucks frozen fish around town. Is that what you want? Think about it."

Ana's mouth falls open, and then fire burns in her eyes. "How can you say such a mean thing to Will? What's wrong with you? Will, I'm so sorry. You just got caught in the middle of something." She turns to Matthew. "I wouldn't go out with you if you were the last guy on Earth!" She goes back into the restaurant.

"You heard her," says Will. "She has no use for you. From now on, you had better leave her alone."

"Look here, little guy," Matthew says. "Don't you ever talk to me like that again.

Will tries to make his face look hard. "This is not about you and me. It's about Ana. She doesn't like you."

Matthew laughs. "Again, little guy? You won't stop. You will never learn. Do I have to hit you?"

"What is your problem, Matthew? What did Ana or I ever do to you?" Will cries out.

"You didn't have to do anything. I just don't like your face," says Matthew. "As for Ana, forget about her and save yourself a world of hurt. Why would she pick you, of all the guys on Earth? I'm the one she really wants. She will come around to me in the end."

4. A Ride Home

In the kitchen, Ana comes to Will and puts her hand on his arm. "Are you all right?"

"Oh, sure. But what about you? That guy Matthew—" He shakes his head.

Ana looks a little sick. "Matthew is harmless, but he sure is full of himself. I'm sorry that he said those things about you. Don't take it hard. You're a great guy."

"I am?" Suddenly Will feels better than all right. "Listen. Anything I can do to help you—"

"I don't need your help, Will. I can take care of myself."

"Are you mad at me?" Will asks.

"No," says Ana. "If anything happened to you, I would be mad at myself. So just stay out of this, OK? It's not your problem."

"Is there a problem? Maybe I can help."

"What could you do?"

"I don't know. The guy doesn't own you, does he? I can't stand to hear him talk to you the way he does."

"I guess that's his way of showing that he likes me," says Ana.

"Some way to show it! Do you like him?" Will knows the answer, but he wants to hear it from her.

Ana, however, doesn't answer the question. "I have to get back to work," she says.

Will thinks maybe he doesn't know the answer after all. *Could it be that Ana does like Matthew?* "Me, too," he says and goes back to get more boxes. Then he heads back to MMF. *So much for my big talk with Ana,* he thinks.

Will's boss, Lou, is waiting for him outside the building. "What took you so long?" The little man looks at his watch. "I hope you didn't have an accident."

"No." Will smiles. "Nothing like that. I just started late. Things just got in the way. Sorry."

"What else?" says his boss.

"What?"

"Something happened to you, Will. I can see it in your eyes. What was it?"

"I was caught in the middle of an argument."

Lou looks him up and down. "You don't **have** to give me the details." He waits. Will says nothing. "I guess I won't push you," Lou says at last. "My door is open if you want to talk. I just hope you did what was right. I had to break up a fight or two in my day. If I ever saw a big guy picking on a little guy—" He stops. He has seen something on Will's face. "What? You think I must have been too little to break up any fights? Don't kid yourself. I could never stand by and let some big guy pick on a little guy. Was it something like that, this fight? Did you stand up for some little guy?"

"Something like that."

"Well, stand up for what's right, and you can't go wrong, I always say. But next time you're going to be late, give me a call, will you?"

"Sorry, Lou. I didn't mean to let you down."

"I know you didn't. You're a good kid, Will. That's why I want you to do something for me. Your truck needs some work. The guy at my shop says he will do it tonight if I can get it there by 10:00. Could you drive the truck over there for me? It's 3604 Arizona. You would have to take the bus home."

"No problem, boss."

"Don't call me boss. It's Lou—just Lou."

Will drives away, feeling happy. The shop is on the north side of town. He will have to go right past the Sea House again. Why that should make him happy, he doesn't know. But as he gets close to the place, he starts to sing.

It's an old song, but he likes it. Then he sees her. Who is that walking down the street? It looks like Ana. Will pulls over. It is Ana. He calls out to her.

She sees him and smiles. "Will!"

"Where are you going?" says Will. "Can I give you a ride?"

Ana shakes her head. "I'm going home. I wouldn't put you to any trouble."

"No trouble. Get in."

"All right." She gets into the truck.

"Where to?" he asks.

"I live at the corner of 19th and Wood," she says. "Do you know where that is?"

"Oh, yes. I have to know my way around the whole city for my job." He pulls into the street and starts driving. Here he is alone with Ana, and he can't think of a thing to say. At last, he cries out, "Did Matthew—"

But she cuts him off. "Let's not talk about Matthew."

"All right." Says Will. "What should we talk about?"

"Anything but him," she says.

Will doesn't care what they talk about as long as they talk. "How is your job?"

"My job has good and bad points," she says. "I need the money, that's why I work. What about you? How's your job?"

"I like my job," says Will. "I drive this truck around and meet people. It's great when I meet people like you." He looks at her out of the corner of his eye. But she seems lost in thought. Did she even hear what he said?

"What about the pay?" she asks suddenly.

"What? Oh, not great." The question makes him feel small.

Her face turns red. "I should not ask a question like that. I'm sorry. Money is on my mind."

"I know what you mean," says Will. "Money is a problem for everyone. I'm trying to save enough to buy a car."

"What's wrong with this truck?"

"Oh, this doesn't belong to me. It goes with the job. Tonight I'm taking it to the shop for my boss. But I can't drive it home most days. I want a car of my own."

"I can understand that," says Ana.

"How about you?" he says. He just wants to keep the talk going. "Do you save your money? What would you like to buy?"

"Right now," says Ana, "I would be happy just to make the rent."

"The rent! But don't you live with your family?"

She gives him a sad smile. "Yes. But I have a big family, and someone has to pay the rent. All of us work one way or another, but it doesn't come to much. My dad doesn't have a real job. He has been looking ever since we got to this country, but so far—nothing. My dad does what he can. He stands outside a food shop and helps people take their bags to their cars. They give him a little something. Now my mom is sick."

"I'm sorry. Is she bad?"

"She will get better. But she lost her job—just as our rent went up. I think we're going to be about $200 short this time. We have to cut back on something." Ana turns to him. "But I should not be telling you all these things. It is not fair. You have a good life. You should not have to think about such problems."

"So your family is new in this country?" Will asks.

"Two years," she says. "Is that new?"

"Why did you leave your country?"

"The war," she says. "The violence. Any time of the night or day, you might hear a gun going off. That's how my little sister was killed. She just happened to be in the wrong place at the wrong time. Someone fired at someone, and she was hit. She was only two years old. We were scared all the time, and we were poor. Here we are only poor. But someday we may not be so poor."

Will has heard stories like Ana's on TV. But they never interested him before. When news about trouble in some other country came up on TV, he would turn to something else. Now he thinks, *Those were real people in those news stories, people like Ana.* Suddenly he has so many questions. "But why—"

But Ana sits up now. "Here it is," she says.

"This is your building?" Will pulls up. The building she has pointed out is not pretty. The paint has cracks. There is graffiti all over the walls. He can hear someone screaming inside. It looks more like a homeless shelter than an apartment building.

But Ana just says, "Good night," and runs to the front door. There she turns and waves before she goes inside.

5. Stolen Money

When Will walks into the Sea House on the following Saturday, he can tell something is wrong. The workers are all standing in the main room, looking scared. Mr. Henson is walking around in a circle, wearing a hard look. Mrs. White just looks helpless.

Will asks one of the workers, "What's going on?"

"Money has been stolen," she tells him.

Suddenly Henson turns to the line of workers. "One of you took this money," he says. "That's what really hurts me—not the $200, but that it was one of you!" Then he pulls his mouth into a small smile. "You thought you could get away with it. But no. I'm going to find out which one of you it is."

"Mr. Henson—"

"What?" The boss turns to Mrs. White.

"These are good people. I work with them every day. Maybe you're getting a little ahead of yourself," she says. "After all, it could have been someone off the street. How do we know—"

Mr. Henson cuts her short. "Fair question. I'll tell you how. Someone from the outside would have to break in. Do you see anything wrong with the doors or windows? I don't. Maybe I don't see as well as I used to. Matthew, look at those doors and windows again for me. Mrs. White says I'm getting old and don't see as well as I used to. Mrs. White doesn't believe—"

"It's not that!" she cries. Her hands are moving. It looks as if she is washing her hands over and over. "It's just that anything could happen—"

"Not in this restaurant, Mrs. White. Here, **anything** doesn't happen," Mr. Henson tells her. "You see, last week I had a lock shop come in and put in a little something for me. This little something calls the police if anyone tries to get in after we close. I didn't say break in—I said get in. Anything will trip this thing. Anything sets it off— anything that anyone might stick into the lock."

"You never told me about this!"

"Why would I, Mrs. White? You didn't need to know," says Mr. Henson. "I thought keeping this thing a secret might pay off. Now I can be sure that no one got in from the outside. So the thief must have been one of my own workers."

"Mr. Henson!" cries Mrs. White. "I hope you're not saying—"

"I'm not saying anything," said Mr. Henson. "Let's just begin at the beginning." He goes to the first worker in the line. "You. When did you leave?" he asks. When he gets the answer, he turns to the others. "Did anyone see him?" When someone says "Yes," he goes to that worker. The questions go on till, at last, he comes to a stop in front of the head cook. "All right, Matthew. Let's have it," says Mr. Henson. "When did you leave last night?"

"Me?" Matthew just has to smile.

"I have to ask everyone," says Mr. Henson. "Of course, you wouldn't steal from this place. But answer the question."

"Let's see. I cooked the last dinner myself. It went out around 10:00. I left right after that," says Matthew.

"Anyone see him leave?" The boss turns to the other workers.

Ana raises her hand. "Well, yes. He stopped to give me some directions. I saw him go out the door."

Then Henson turns to Mrs. White. "Was the money in the till when Matthew left?"

"Yes, it was."

"So it's down to you and this girl." He points to Ana. "What can you tell us, Mrs. White? Aren't you always the last to leave?"

"Well, most of the time. But last night I was feeling a little sick. I left around 11:00."

"Who was here at the time?"

"Just Ana. She still had some work to do for Matthew. I told her to turn out the lights. The door does lock by itself, you know. So I thought it would be OK if—"

"Now we're getting somewhere." Mr. Henson turns to Ana. "Now I think I see it all. Mrs. White took off, and you were here by yourself. Is that about right?"

Will feels something inside him turning to ice. He sees it, too. He sees it better than Mr. Henson, in fact. He knows how badly Ana needed money, and $200 is just how much she needed! She has stolen it from her boss. That is really bad. Yet, Will can't help but feel sorry for her.

Then Will has an idea—a way to buy Ana some time. She won't know what he's doing. He will tell her later. Right now, he just has to do something fast. Ana is standing there with scared eyes like some night creature caught in the lights of a car.

Mr. Henson opens his mouth. But Will cuts in before he can get a word out. "May I say something?"

Mr. Henson looks around. "Who are you?"

"He works for Mississippi Meat and Fish," says Matthew.

"We don't have time for you now," says Mr. Henson.

"I think you do want to hear from me right now. I may know something about all this."

"Well?" says Mr. Henson. "What is it?"

"I saw a guy—" Will says.

"What guy?" the boss says.

"What guy?" Matthew wants to know.

"Just some guy," says Will. "Never mind the details. I just have an idea he might have been interested in this place. I may know some people who know him."

"You didn't listen, boy. I just told everyone," Mr. Henson says. "No one could get in from the outside because—"

"Forget that, Mr. Henson. Anything some lock shop puts in, someone somewhere can crack," Will says.

"You know a lot about this kind of thing, do you?" Mr. Henson gives him a close look.

"No, but I hear things. I read about this one thief in the paper. He worked in a lock shop. He would put in a lock. That night, he would break into the place. Maybe something like that happened to you."

"Maybe. I can't put **maybe** in the bank," says Mr. Henson.

"But you can turn **maybe** over to the cops." says Will.

"Hey!" Mr. Henson gets mad. "Are you talking back to me?"

"I don't take orders from you," says Will. "I don't work for you, Mr. Henson. I'm trying to help you. Just hold off on calling anyone a thief for a day or two. Let me ask around, see what I can find out. Maybe I can even get your money back."

"I'll believe that when I see it," says Mr. Henson.

"Give me two days," says Will. "Just two days."

6. People Will Talk

Now why did I do that? Will asks himself as he drives away from the Sea House. *What am I going to do? How am I going to get that money?*

He knows the answer. He just doesn't like it much, now that he thinks about it. He will have to take some of his own money out of the bank. *It won't be like losing the money,* he thinks. *Ana will pay me back when she can.* But he knows that will not be soon. If she had the money now, she would not have stolen it.

The banks are open on Saturdays till 12:00. He takes the $200 out. The woman at the window counts out the money without any questions. She pushes the bills across to him. Then she gives him a paper that shows how much he has left: $200. That sure looks small after the $400 he used to have. *Oh, well,* he tells himself. *It's worth it. Now Ana will know how strongly I feel about her. We'll talk about it over dinner.* Pictures of that dinner go through his mind. He and Ana are sitting across from each other holding hands. She is looking into his eyes. After dinner, they get into his car—but wait. What car? He won't have any kind of car for a long time. The thought is like cold water.

Mr. Henson is waiting for him at the Sea House. Will walks right up to the man. "Here you go, Mr. Henson. I told you I might get your money back, and I did it." Will looks around. He wants to make sure everyone sees him do this. In fact, everyone does stop working to watch as he hands the money over.

Mr. Henson counts it and puts it in his pocket. "It's all here," he says. "I will let it go this time. But you go and tell your friend—"

"He's not my friend," says Will.

"Well, whatever he is," says the boss.

Will goes past Mr. Henson. Out of the corner of his eye, he sees Matthew talking to him. Only a few of the words reach Will. "I'm telling you, Henson, keep an eye on Will," Matthew says.

"I'm way ahead of you," says Henson.

The words make Will mad. People will talk. He can't stop them. They can't prove anything. He finds Ana in the kitchen. Her eyes are red, as if she has been crying.

"How do you feel?" he says.

"Not well," she says.

"You should go home," says Will. "You've been through so much. Take the rest of the day off."

"I have to work," she says in a cold voice. "I need the money."

"Take a sick day. Mr. Henson will understand, won't he? I've got the truck outside. I could give you a ride home." He is thinking, *We can talk on the ride home.*

Ana just shakes her head. "I can get home by myself."

"I just—" The words are hard to get out. "I just wanted to do something for you."

"Don't you think you've done enough?" says Ana.

"What?" He's not sure he heard her right. "What does that mean?"

"Never mind." Ana turns away. "What right do I have to say anything to you?"

"Yes, really! What right—" He stops before he says something he will be sorry about later. He is mad at Ana. The others, he can understand. They don't know who really took the money. Ana is different. Why is she talking to him this way, and after what he has done for her! Maybe she doesn't know what he has done. He says, "You do know that I gave Mr. Henson $200, don't you? Aren't you happy with me for doing that?"

"I'm happy that you did that. Yes." She sounds sad.

"Well, I should hope so! I should think you would be very happy about that!" Will's mind is going in a circle. Is Ana going to say she didn't steal the money? He can't prove she did or make her pay him back. He will just be out $200. Never did he think she would do such a thing. Now, for the first time, he sees that he could have been wrong about Ana. After all, what does he really know about her? She keeps to herself. She has a pretty face. What does that add up to? Not much.

7. A Word With Lou

Will is mad all that day. He is mad the next day, too. He never wants to see Ana again. He wants to see her right away. He wants to get in her face and scream, "How could you do this to me?" He wants to take her in his arms and say, "You and me. Somehow we will work through this together."

Every day he hopes to see Sea House written on his card. Then he remembers what happened there, and he says to himself, *I am never going back to the Sea House. The next time they want something, I'll tell Lou no way. Get someone else.* But the days go by without an order from the Sea House. This, too, makes him mad. How can he turn them down if they never ask?

Then one day, when he gets to work, he is told that Lou wants to see him. "About what?" he asks, but the guys don't know. So Will heads up the stairs. He doesn't know why, but he feels scared. He stops just inside the room. "You wanted to see me, Lou?"

"Yes, Will. Sit down," says Lou. "The Sea House called today."

"Yes?" Will can feel everything inside him falling.

"They want four boxes of fish and two of meat," says Lou.

"OK." Will starts to get up.

"But," says Lou, "they don't want you."

"What?" Will falls back.

"They asked me to have some other guy stop by with it. Any other guy, in fact."

"What's wrong with me?" says Will.

"They wouldn't tell me," says Lou. "I asked. I said, 'Hey! You got something against one of my boys, put it out where I can see it.' But they wouldn't come clean. In the end, they just said, 'OK. You're right. We can't prove anything. Forget it.' So now I'm asking you, Will. What happened over there?"

"Who did you talk to from the Sea House, Lou? Was it the cook? A guy named Matthew?"

"That's him," said Lou.

"Well, the first thing you should know is he has something against me. He would do anything to get me in trouble."

"Why is that, Will?"

Will says nothing for a long time.

His boss asks again. "Why does the cook feel that way about you, Will?"

"Well," says Will, "I like this girl who works at the Sea House. Matthew likes her, too."

"I see," says Lou. "This whole thing is about a girl?"

"Not all of it," says Will.

"Go on," says Lou.

"The other night someone took money from the Sea House."

Lou raises his head. "Oh. That's bad," he says. "How much?"

"About $200," says Will.

"What does this have to do with you?" asks Lou.

"I told them I might know who did it. Then I gave Mr. Henson $200."

"You gave Henson $200?" cries Lou. "Where did you get it?"

"From the bank. It was money I had saved up. Now I think Matthew is telling everyone I was the one who took the money in the first place."

"Hold on." Lou raises his hand. "Let me see if I get this. You didn't steal the money and had nothing to do with it. But you took out $200 of your own money and gave it to this Henson character. Now, why would you do that?" Lou looks at Will and waits.

Will looks back at Lou. "Believe me, Lou. I know what you're thinking. But you're wrong. I didn't steal anything from this restaurant."

"OK. If you say so, I believe you, Will. I know you, and this whole thing doesn't add up. Why would you steal the money one day and give it back the next? But you still have not answered my question. Why did you give Mr. Henson this money if you were not the thief?"

"I was trying to keep someone else out of trouble."

"So you know who did steal this money?"

"Yes, I think so."

"Well now, Will. This is different. You said you had nothing to do with this. But knowing who did it puts you right in the middle. Who was it?"

"I don't know if I should tell you, Lou. It isn't my secret to give away. If anyone tells, it should be the thief. That's my feeling. Do you see my point, Lou?"

"Yes, but it's such a little point," says Lou. "It's good that you want to help your friend. That's coming from the good in you. But what are you doing when you keep this secret? Give it some long, hard thought, Will. What are you really doing? You're helping your friend get away with it. Think about it. If someone steals and gets away with it, what are they going to do? Steal again, if you ask me. So what are you really doing by keeping this secret? You're helping to turn your friend into a real thief—for life."

"I just don't know what to do, Lou. This is hard for me."

"Why not just tell Mr. Henson who really took the money?"

"You don't know him."

"Oh! You mean he's not such a great guy. Is that it? Does that mean it's OK to steal from him?"

"No! It's just that I know this girl isn't really a thief. She has problems. I think she was feeling pushed. She lost her head and made a wrong move. Mr. Henson will never see that—or care. He will just turn her over to the cops and ruin her life."

"Her? We're talking about a girl here? I think I see the whole picture now."

Will closes his mouth. He has said too much.

"Listen," says Lou, "you're the one who has to make this whole thing right. You know that, don't you? At this point, it's not up to you. Talk to the girl. That's first. I don't know what's going on between you two—"

"Nothing!" cries Will.

"Look, I don't want to know," Lou goes on. "It doesn't change anything. You have to do what's right, Will. Whatever your feelings might be. Get this girl to turn herself in, and don't make any bones about it. Tell her if she doesn't do it, you will. Believe me, in years to come you will both be happy that she did."

"What if she won't?"

"Then you have to follow through. You have to go to whoever—Mr. Henson, the cops, take your pick—but it should not have to come to that. If you like this girl, she must have some good in her. If she has that, she will see your point. If she doesn't see your point, maybe you were wrong about her in the first place. Just remember one thing."

"What's that, Lou?"

"Feelings can throw you off. Don't listen to your feelings," Lou tells him. "Listen to what's right."

"Does it have to be one or the other?" says Will. "Can't your feelings tell you what is right sometimes? My feelings are screaming about this, telling me there is something wrong about turning her in and all. This is hard." Will shakes his head.

"Life is like that," says Lou. He puts his hands together and sits back.

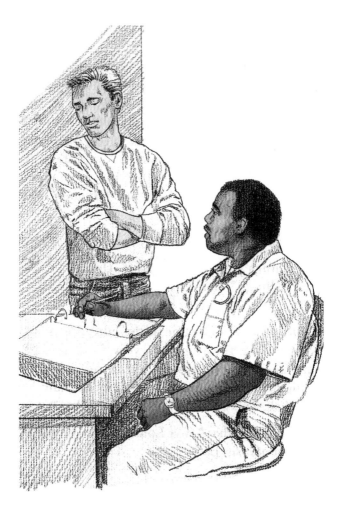

"Feelings can throw you off. Don't listen to your feelings," Lou tells Will. "Listen to what's right."

8. Fire and Ice

Will drives slowly to the Sea House. He finds a place to park. He takes his time getting out. Very slowly he makes his way to the back door. The restaurant is closed today, but Ana will be here. Will knows she will be alone. This may be the only time he will have to talk to her.

The back door is not locked. He sticks his head inside. "Anyone here?" he calls. No one answers. He walks in. He makes his way around the big freezer and sees Ana at the far end of the kitchen.

"Will!" She starts to smile, but then the smile turns cold. "What are you doing here?"

"I needed to talk to you."

"About what?" she asks.

"About the money that was stolen."

"I don't want to hear it, Will. This is just too hard for me."

"You have to listen to me, Ana."

"Why me? Why don't you go right to Mr. Henson? Or to Mrs. White? Or even to Matthew?"

"Why would I talk to those people before I talk to you?" Will cries out. "What kind of guy do you think I am?"

"What?" she says.

"You should be the one to talk to them. It wouldn't be the same if I went. Go to Mr. Henson, if you think that's best. Or right to the cops—in the end, that might be better."

"The cops!" she cries out. "You really want **me** to go to the cops?"

"You have to do what's right," he says. "Look, I think it will be OK. People understand what it's like to have problems."

"What problems do you have?" she says. "You tell me you want to buy a car so you can take some girl out. Is a problem like that worth—"

"Let's leave my problems out of this. It's your problems we're talking about."

"My problems?" She gives him the eye. "Why my problems?"

"What?" he says.

"What?" she says. Then they both stop talking and just stand face to face, saying nothing. Suddenly she raises her head. "What's that?"

"What?" he asks.

"That sound," she says. "Don't you hear it?"

He can hear something. "It sounds like cars on the freeway."

"Only there is no freeway around here," she says.

"No, I was wrong," he says. "It sounds more like the sea."

"We're miles from the sea," she points out.

Will goes to the back door and looks out. "There is nothing in the street," he says. He comes back to Ana in the middle of the kitchen. "This is where I hear it best. Could it be in the walls?"

Ana puts her hand against the wall. "Oh, no. Feel this."

Will feels the wall. "It's hot!"

He and Ana look at each other. "There must be a fire in there," says Ana.

"Let's get out of here," says Will. "Come on."

"Wait," says Ana. "I have to do something first."

"No time," he says. "You can do it later."

"No," she says. "I can't just leave if there is a fire in the restaurant. I have to call someone. But there is no telephone on the street around here. Who knows how far we might have to drive! Do you have the truck?"

"Yes! I have the truck. Believe me, Ana, there is no time for this. Everything I've ever heard says to get out right away when there is a fire." Will tries to take her hand.

"This will not take long," Ana says. She is already calling. He can't leave her here. Now she has gotten through to someone. She is talking.

Then, suddenly, the fire is in the room with them. It is as if some big red monster has come through the wall. It screams and turns. The telephone falls out of Ana's hand. Will backs away from the fire, feeling the heat on his face. Some wooden boxes against the wall go up. Just like that a wall of fire stands between Will and the back door.

Then, suddenly, the fire is in the room with them.

"We have to go out the front," screams Ana.

Hand in hand, they race to the front door. Ana turns the handle and pulls, and she pulls again. The door will not open! "Oh, no! Oh, no!" She looks at Will. "How could I forget?"

"What?" he says.

"Mr. Henson changed the lock," she says. "We can't get it open from the inside."

"We have to break a window," he says. "Find something we can throw." But then it's already too late for even that. The fire has followed them to the front door.

Ana and Will are cut off from the front and cut off from the back. They can only move to the middle of the kitchen, and that space keeps getting smaller.

"Oh, Will!" Ana sounds scared. "We should have gotten out when you said."

"Never mind that now. We have to think of something." Will knows his voice is shaking, but he doesn't care.

"It's no use," she says. "We're going to die here. We have no place left to go. We're caught."

Then the idea comes to him. "There is one place."

"Where?" asks Ana.

"Here." Will pulls the door of the freezer open. He pushes Ana in and follows her, then pulls the door shut.

The freezer is a little room with no windows. As soon as the door closes, they can no longer feel the heat or hear the fire. The light goes out as soon as the door closes. But Ana turns it back on from the inside. "Are we safe in here?" she asks.

"These walls were made to keep in the cold," says Will. "They should keep out the heat, too. We will be safe—for awhile."

"Cold," says Ana, "but safe."

Big sides of frozen meat hang along one wall. Boxes of frozen fish line the other wall. Will puts three of the boxes one on top of another and sits down on them. Ana just stands.

They say nothing to each other for awhile. Both are lost in thought. But then Will has to move. He can't stay in the same place very long. It's too cold. Ana smiles. She knows why he is moving. She is sitting down now, and she has picked her feet up off the floor. "Cold," she says. "I'm just happy that it isn't dark as well."

Just then the light goes out.

Ana lets out a little cry. Will asks, "What happened?"

"The fire must have gotten to the electricity," she says. "Will, I don't know if I can stand sitting here in the dark very long. How will we know when it's safe to go out?"

"It might be safe now," says Will. "Should I stick my head out and take a look?" He feels his way to the door and finds the cold metal handle. But he can't move it. "Ana?"

"Yes, Will?"

"Do you know how to get this door open?"

"I've never had to open it from the inside before," she says. "But there must be a way. Let me try."

He can feel when she comes up next to him. He helps her find the door handle. Then she pulls and pushes on it. Nothing happens, and after awhile she stops trying. "I think I know what happened."

"Is it bad?" he wants to know.

"This whole freezer runs on electricity," she says. "Every part of it. Even the door handle."

"You mean if the electricity goes out—"

"The door won't open," she says.

9. In the Freezer

Will starts to laugh.

"What's the big joke?" she wants to know.

"We're going to die of cold in the middle of a fire," he says. "An all-time first, I'm sure. Are you scared?" he asks.

"Yes," she says. "Aren't you?"

"Very. But we'll make it, Ana. I just know we will."

"I called for the firetrucks. I'm not sure how much I got across. By then the fire was in the room with us."

"They must have heard you scream. Believe me, Ana, something got across. All we have to do is wait."

"How long?" she says. "I'm so cold."

"Come here, then." Will can hardly believe he is saying this. "Sit next to me." Then he puts his arms around Ana and holds her close. "Don't take this the wrong way," he feels the need to add. "It's not what you think."

"I know," she says. "We have to hold each other if we want to get out of here alive. We have to hold each other close."

And so they do.

After awhile, there in the dark, she says, "I always liked you, Will. Why did you have to steal that money?"

"What?" He pulls away from her.

"You know—the restaurant money," she says. "Why?"

"Ana! You of all people should know! I never took that money. You know good and well that—"

"Oh, Will. Here we are alone in this freezer, and maybe we're going to die. You're not going to tell me that same old story again about the guy from the street—"

"Ana! Stop!" He cuts her off. "Why are you doing this? You know who took the money, and so do I."

"Who?"

"Well—you did, didn't you? Look, I know what pushed you into it. You were scared. You thought your family would be out on the street. I'm sure you thought you were going to put it all back somehow before—"

"Hey! Are you calling me a thief? What gives you the right?"

"I don't want to. But you took—"

"You took the money! Everyone says so."

"You believe them? I can't call you a thief, but you can call me one? Somehow that's OK?"

That makes her stop and think. After awhile, she says, "Really? Do you mean this? You didn't steal the money?"

"No way! Didn't you?"

"Never. But Will—you did give Mr. Henson $200. Where did that money come from?"

So he tells her. "Out of my bank. It was some of my own money I had saved to buy a car!"

"Why did you give it to Mr. Henson?"

"To save you! Don't you know?" he says. "Mr. Henson was about to call you a thief and turn you over to the cops. You were in the restaurant that night. You were alone. You needed $200. You help Mrs. White count the money. The **when**, the **why**, and the **how**—it was all in place. I thought even if you did it, you were sorry. You would fix it if you could. But Mr. Henson would never let you. He would ruin your life without looking back. That's how it looked to me, and I couldn't let that happen. I just had to give you another crack at doing the right thing. So I made up the story that no one believes. It was the best I could come up with right then and there."

"You did all that for me?" says Ana. "Why?"

"Because I like you," Will tells her. "Because— what can I say? Maybe I am a little in love with you."

She lets out a short laugh. "What a great time to find this out. Will, I wouldn't steal to get out of trouble. I'm not that kind of girl. Now come back here and put your arms around me."

"You're still cold?"

"No—yes—I don't know. That's not why. I just want you to hold me."

"Because you like me?" he wants to know.

"Will," she answers him, "I have liked you since the first time I saw you, if you really want to know."

"Does this mean you will go out with me sometime?"

"Right now," she says. "Do you know of a way out?"

They both laugh.

"How long do you think we have been in here?" she asks after awhile.

"It's so hard to tell," he answers. "Time goes so slow in a place like this—scared like we are— just waiting."

"So it does." She sounds sad. "I would give anything to know what time it is."

"Don't you have a watch?"

"Sure," she says. "So what? I can't see it."

"Wait. I think I have a light somewhere." Will feels around in his pocket. "Here. Let me strike it for you. Get your watch ready. It won't last long."

As the little fire comes up, he sees her face in the red light. She isn't looking at her watch. A paper has caught her eye. It must have fallen out of Will's pocket. It's on the floor. Ana reads out what is written there: "555–7670." She says, "What is this, Will?"

"Never mind. That's just someone I was going to call. What does your watch say?"

"3:30," she answers, as the fire goes out. "Why were you going to call Matthew?"

"Matthew? How did Matthew come up?" Then suddenly Will sees. "You mean the paper that came out of my pocket? That was Matthew's telephone number?"

"Yes. I have to call him about work sometimes. It's not his house, but it's one of the places I can reach him."

Will says, "I was told to call that place to buy a guitar. Turns out it was a stolen guitar, so I never called."

"A stolen guitar?" she says. "Why would Matthew have a stolen guitar?"

"Good question." Will's mind has started to race.

"You know what it makes me think?" says Ana. "It makes me think, if you didn't steal that money—"

"I know."

"I didn't steal it—"

"I know what you're going to say."

But she says it anyway. "Who did steal that money?"

10. Singing in the Dark

"It was Matthew," says Will. "It had to be."

"But it couldn't have been," says Ana. "It's not that I'm taking his side. I just know that he was gone by 10:30 that night. The thief had to be someone who was there that night."

"Did it?" Will is excited suddenly. "I'm not so sure. Tell me about that night again. He was gone by 10:30, you say?"

"Yes. I saw him leave," says Ana. "He gave me a whole lot of work to finish. Then he took a drink down to Mrs. White. Then he left. Everyone saw him go—I wasn't the only one."

"Of course they did," says Will. "He made a big noise about it, in fact. He wanted everyone to know when he **left**. You know why? So that no one would think about when he came **back**! Who says the money was stolen that night? We're all used to thinking of a thief as someone who works at night. But Matthew was alone in the restaurant **the next day**. He could have stolen the money then!"

"Why would he?" says Ana.

"Why? It was the money. Money can buy things, and things are what Matthew likes. What's to understand?"

"Yes, but Matthew is rich. You should see how he throws money around."

"I've seen it," says Will. "I want to know how come he has so much of it to throw around."

"He's the head cook. He makes good money."

"But does he make that much? His new car is worth more money than I'll ever make. He has a boat. His CD player is worth more than any car I could buy. No, I don't think Matthew makes all that money from his job."

"You mean he's a thief?" says Ana. "Even if that is so, why would he steal $200 from this restaurant? That's just change to a guy like him."

"I see your point. Maybe this time he didn't steal for the money. Maybe he did it to get back at you."

"Me!" This rocks Ana.

"Think about it," says Will. "What did he do just before he left? He gave you some work that would keep you late. Then he gave Mrs. White a drink, you said. Soon after that she started to feel so sick she had to go home early. Matthew set you up—don't you see? He made sure that you would be alone in the restaurant that night. The next day he came in, and he took the money, knowing it would look like you did it. The whole thing was a plot, Ana, to make you look bad."

"Only it didn't work because of you," says Ana.

"Which is why Matthew turned it around." Will gets the whole picture at last. "If he couldn't get you, he would get me. He was mad at both of us, after all. Do you know that he called my boss and tried to have me fired? It's a good thing Lou is so cool."

"Well," says Ana, "we worked that one out. What do we do next? I tell you, we have to do something. I don't mean about Matthew. I mean about being in here. This darkness is getting to me. I am starting to see pictures in my head."

"I know," says Will. "It feels like it's been a year."

"We could sing," she says, "to pass the time. Do you know this one?" She starts to sing. The voice that comes out of that darkness makes Will's eyes water. It cuts right to his bones. He has never heard anything like it.

"Down by the banks—of the green, green sea," she sings. "Down by the sea—you and me—you and me—" She turns in his arms. "Do you know that one?"

"Ana, where in the world did you learn to sing like that?" He lets the words out slowly.

"From the radio?" She laughs. "I don't know. Who has to learn? I just love to sing. Do I sing different from anyone else?"

"Better, Ana. You sing better than anyone I have ever heard."

"You like my voice?"

"I like your voice, the way you sing the words— everything about you," says Will.

"Well, then, sing with me. Let's think of a song we both know."

"Believe me, you won't like hearing my voice."

"Oh, come on! How bad could it be?"

"Well," he says, "just to give you an idea, my band is called The Sick Dogs."

"Your band?"

"That's just a joke. It's not really a band. Just three guys and me. We get together and play sometimes. Ana, you're cold again. I can feel you shaking," says Will.

"I'm not cold. I just feel a little sick. Can darkness make you sick? I feel like I might pass out."

"I hope we're not getting short on air."

"Air," says Ana. "Oh, no. I didn't think about that. The air could run out. If the cold doesn't get us—"

"There must be someone out there by now," says Will. "How long does it take them to get to a fire?"

"Will," she says, "I just thought of something bad. What if they put out the fire and went home already? Why would anyone look in the freezer? No one knows we're here."

"No," he says, "Ana, it can't be. They are out there now."

"Then let's make noise," says Ana. "We have to let them know we are in here. Let's both scream at the same time—"

"No one will hear that. These freezer walls are solid. It's like we're inside a mountain."

"Then let's hit something against the walls. Sound goes through solid metal."

"We could try it." Suddenly Will's head feels like it's full of spider webs. They are in his eyes. They are in his mouth. Yes, the air must be running out. He shakes his head hard, trying to get the webs out. "We need something harder than my hand. It has to be something like a rock—"

"How about this?" She pushes a big frozen fish into his hand.

"This should do it," he says. "Stand back, Ana. I don't want to hit you." Ana gets out of the way, and Will goes to work. *Smash* goes the big fish against the wall.

"Again!" cries Ana.

Will keeps hitting. The fish is like a stick of ice. His hands feel like ice, too. But he doesn't let up till the last frozen fish cracks and falls apart.

11. A New Life

Then it happens. The door opens. Light comes in. Two men walk into the freezer. One of them is a cop. The other looks like the fire chief. Will is so cold he can hardly move. The men help him out. Ana walks out on her own and then falls over. She lands in water that is all over the floor. Someone helps her back up and puts a blanket around her. The restaurant is dark, and the fire is out, but the walls are not yet cool. The wall between the kitchen and the front room is just one big hole. The front room is a ruin. The front windows are gone. Will sees glass all over the floor.

Mrs. White is at the restaurant. So is Mr. Henson. The cop has a book out. He is asking questions and writing down answers. The fire chief is in the back, giving directions to his crew. Mrs. White tells the cop, "Don't ask me. Ask her. She was here when the fire started."

Will and Ana after the fire.

The cop turns to Ana with his questions. She tells him everything she knows. Mr. Henson stands behind her with a long face. Ana describes the front door that wouldn't open. "It had a new lock, you see. It doesn't open from the inside." The fire chief hears this and comes over.

"A new lock?" he says to Mr. Henson. "You put in a lock that can't be opened from the inside? That's against the law."

"Look," says Henson, "don't talk to me about the law. I have people breaking in here right and left taking my money. I had to do something."

"This girl came close to losing her life because of your lock," the fire chief says. "That boy, too."

"Hey, wait a minute. Now I'm sorry about that—" Mr. Henson's face has suddenly gone white.

Ana says. "Forget about all that for now. I want to talk about the money that was stolen the other night. Mr. Henson, the guy who took that money was Matthew."

"Matthew?" Mr. Henson says laughing.

"Oh, Ana. What a thing to say!" Mrs. White gives her a helpless look and starts washing her hands. "Matthew is our head cook. He's not a thief."

At these words, the cop raises his head. "Cook?" he says. "Thief? Your head cook is a thief?"

"No! She said he's not a thief, he's a cook!" Mr. Henson cries out.

"He's both," says Will. "He had a stolen guitar for sale a few weeks back. I hear he has stolen things for sale all the time."

"A thief and a cook," says the cop. "You know— I saw something just the other day—what was it? Oh, yes. I remember now. A cook from California." He turns to Mrs. White. "Tell me about your cook again. What is his name?"

"Matthew. But why—"

"Where is this Matthew now?" the cop wants to know.

"Well, he's at home, I should think. Why?"

"What does he look like? Do you have a picture of him?"

"Yes. I have one right here." She takes a picture of all the people who work at the restaurant to the cop. "This is him in the middle. Why do you want to know?"

The cop doesn't answer. He is looking at the picture. "Boy," he says, "that does look like him, all right. It isn't a face you forget."

"Why on Earth are you so interested in Matthew?" says Mrs. White.

"His name isn't really Matthew. It's Robert. Robert Water. He's wanted in California. We got the facts on him last week. He's a thief. No, more than a thief. He runs a ring, or he did out in California anyway. He had a gang working for him. His gang would break into cars, houses—you name it."

"I can't believe it," says Mrs. White. "If he's a thief, how come he works here—as a cook?"

"Oh, but he's not just any old cook, is he?" The cop laughs. "He's the head cook—at the best place in town. That's his other side. He thinks of himself as a great cook. I guess he's not the only one who thinks so. He used to run a famous restaurant in California. Famous because of him, from what I hear. Big stars used to fight to get into the place. Then the cops found out about his other side—the outlaw side. They went to pick him up, but he was gone. The trouble is, this guy likes to cook. He likes to steal, but he likes to cook, too. He can't stay away from either one.

The first time he got away, he turned up in Arizona—working as a cook—not just at any old place. No—at the best place in town. He was making a name for himself there—a new name, you might say. But he was a head thief again, too, running a new ring. Again he got away before the cops could pick him up. After that, everyone thought he would stay away from restaurant work. But no—here he is again." The cop shakes his head. "Some people never learn."

"He is a very good cook," says Mrs. White.

"So I hear," said the cop. "I guess there is some good in everyone. I'm going to call the chief on this right away. We can't let this man get away again."

Mr. Henson isn't saying much now. He seems to know that he looks pretty bad. Just a few days back, he was calling everyone in the restaurant a thief—everyone but Matthew. Now it turns out Matthew was the only thief.

"Well," says Mrs. White, "now we have new problems. We are going to need a new head cook when we open up again. We can move Tom up, of course, and put Luis in Tom's place. Then we're going to need someone to take Luis's place."

"Ana can cook," says Will.

"She's too young." Mrs. White looks at the girl. "We need a good cook."

"I have been helping Matthew," Ana says. "I know how to cook every dish."

"Maybe you should give her the job," says Will.

Mr. Henson turns and says to Will, "You keep out of this, boy. So, you know how to cook?" he says to Ana. "That's all well and good. How much money do you want?"

"How much did Luis make?"

"I can't give you that much," Mr. Henson screams. "Luis has been to cooking school."

Will says, "Why don't you let her try? If she can't do it, look for someone else. One thing you have to say—Ana's not a thief."

"Well, that is worth something," says Henson. He thinks it over and then he says, "All right, Ana, you have a new job. Now, how about you?" He turns to Will. "Do you want a new job?"

"No. But what did you have in mind?"

"You can take over for Ana and work your way up. You caught a thief for me. That gives you points. How much do you make now?"

"I can only work from 3:00 to 7:00, you understand. I still go to school."

"I can live with that. How much do you make?"

"I make $32 a day."

"I'll give you more. Call your boss and tell him. You can use my phone."

Will doesn't really want to work for Mr. Henson. But he thinks, *I could be close to Ana this way.* So he gets Lou on Mr. Henson's car phone. "Hey, Lou. I'm at the Sea House—"

"Good. Did you fix that problem?"

"It's a long story," says Will. "The short answer is yes. Right now, I have to tell you, this man Mr. Henson—"

"Yes, I remember him. The mean guy."

"Right. Well, he wants to give me a job here at the Sea House."

"You don't want to work for that guy, do you?" says Lou.

"No, I like working for you, Lou. But Mr. Henson says he will give me more money."

"How much more?" says Lou.

"Hold on." Will puts the telephone down. He calls to Mr. Henson. "How much are you willing to pay me?"

"What is this?" says Mr. Henson. "Are you trying to hold my feet to the fire? More, that's all I know for now. I'll give you $35 a day. How is that? No—wait. All right. You've talked me into it. Make it $40."

Will turns back to the telephone. "He says he will give me $40 a day, Lou."

"Is that right? Well, I can't let this character steal my best worker, Will. From now on, you get $45 a day working for me. How do you like that?"

"I like it," says Will.

He goes back to Mr. Henson. He says, "Well, I can't take your job. But it was good of you to think of me."

Ana says, "Mr. Henson, Will gave you $200 of his own money. He did it to help me. He thought you were trying to make me out to be the thief."

"Where did he get that idea?" cries Mr. Henson. "I had my eye on Matthew all along."

"If you say so. But Will should get his $200 back."

"Yes, of course," says Mr. Henson. "Just what I was going to say myself. Will, stop by next week."

"Will do, Mr. Henson."

"Just one more thing. No more fish this week. We're going to be closed till we fix the place up again. But Ana—you get full pay till we open again."

He turns and walks away fast.

"I can hardly wait," says Will. He turns to Ana. "The truck is outside. Can I give you a ride home?" Then when they are on the street, he asks, "Ana, what are you doing Saturday night?"

"Well, I'm not working, I guess. Why?"

"I was going to ask—" and then he has an idea. "I'm getting together with some friends. We're going to play music that night. We need a singer. You want to sit in with us? Try us out?"

"I would love to," says Ana. She looks into his face and then takes his hand. Together they make their way to the truck.